The Ones Within

Sean Lause

Acknowledgments

I would like to thank Tom Beery, a better teacher than I, and Will Wells, a better writer than I, for their help with revising and editing these poems.

Poems in The Ones Within have appeared in literary journals, including:

"The man who turned inside-out"—*Acumen, 2River View, Red River Review*

"Imagination longing"—*California Quarterly, Green Hills Literary Lantern, Main Street Rag*

"The night I knocked the world out of loop"—*Spillway*

"Bird in the attic"—*The Deronda Rveiew, Rio Grande Review*

"Journey with no sound"—*Third Wednesday, Poetic Matrix: A Poetic Letter*

"The madman whirling through the tree"—*Van Gogh's Ear*

"The knitter of gentle darkness"—*The New Verse News*

"The wolf as original dreamer"—*Caveat Lector, The Mother Earth International, Line Stars Magazine, Illumen, The King's English*

Nominated for the Pushcart Prize, 2006

"Shadow heart"—*Ancient Paths*

"Double shift"—*Packingtown Review*

"The watcher in the window"—*Struggle*

"My father's cat"—*The Comstock Review*

"Capturing the light"—*The Briar Cliff Review*

"My father's light"—*Small things*

"Inheritance"—*Indefinite Space, The Halcyone Literary Review, The Innisfree Poetry Journal*

"Kite-flying at night"—*Homestead, Lalitamba, Long Story Short, Ascent Aspirations*

"I love the whole world which includes your left shoulder"—*Innisfree Poetry Journal*

"Her night gowns"—*Poets Expresso Review*

"The obscenity of angels"—*Kaleidoscope*

"Awakening the abyss"—

"Walt Whitman at the game"—*Wild Violet, Baseball Bard, The Comstock Review*

"The Eyes of Leo Frank"—*Samsara, Lines*

"Mackley"—*Poetry, Trajectory, Clark Street Review, Raving Dove*

"Charlie Parker Negative"—*Jerry Jazz Musician*

"Diamond of silence"—*The Deronda Review*

"Robert Lowell shops at Sears"—*Pennsylvania English*

"Orphan Day at the Science Marina"—*Struggle*

"Midwest Photographs"—*Backchannels Journal*

"Greyhound Iowa refugee"—*Main Street Rag, Clark Street Review*

"Night fishing in Hog River"—*Struggle*

"Charlottesville"—*Hawaii Pacific Review, The Briar Cliff Review, Nationalism: (Mis)understanding Donald Trump's Capitalism, Racism Global Politics, International Trade and Media Wars* (Mwanaka Media Publishing, 2019).

"End Men Blues"—

"Make America Great Again"—*Coal Hill Review*

Contents

Part Three:
From Walt Whitman's America to Donald Trump's America .

Part One: Colors of the spirit

"Nature always wears the colors of the spirit."

—Ralph Waldo Emerson

The man who turned inside-out

In a sudden wind,
his mind turned inside-out
like an umbrella.
He could feel the spokes of the real
bend, groan and break
like the spine of that umbrella.
He could feel his heart,
his veins, his blood, his breath
as if they were at last his own.
Words beheld the things they imagined.
Poems dropped gently with the leaves,
and books read deep into their readers.
Then another wind
turned the world inside-out
and he blossomed into darkness and light.
He heard stars whisper like children,
the night bless lovers with planets conjoined,
and dandelions chant silver to the moon.
Now he lets storms blow through him,
the sun enlighten him, and the moon dream him
to the silence of his happy bones.

Imagination longing

The moon imagines itself
from silence to an O of wonder,
dreaming of how to spend its silver coin.
The earth is a faithful horse
circling its absent master's house.
The house weeps for the horse down its windows.
The sky is in love with the light it can't hold,
the light with the sun it remembers,
the sun a throbbing vacancy of blue.
Though they burn holes in darkness,
the stars forever shiver. The darkness
is a door longing for a key.
Planets ripen for a harvest
that never comes. Each dreams a world
beyond the endless zero of its sum.
One child day I tore a flower free,
and toppled from the all of holiness,
till I learned to bless the shadows of the Fall.

The night I knocked the world out of loop

I had waited eternity
for this chance. Observatory.
My childhood bed, ordered
phosphorescent universe
that my father glued to my ceiling
at last to glow to life.
But I banged my head
on the reflector, and stagger-
dazed into the night. When I
gazed high the constellations
came unglued, the heavens, disastered,
rattled their nervous jewels.
Then I fell in fear and wonder
through endless unchartered light.
New worlds glittered their clarity—
pebbles beneath a frozen stream,
while galaxy stallions
whirled and plunged their manes.
Now I was free to touch the silence!
Or speak the words of diamonds, watch
planets whir like tops cupped in palms.
And then I saw—Venus and Mars—
like ripe berries
twined round a branch of stars.

Kaleidoscope boy

First he took the wound of names
and wound them round a dawn.
He gathered light in his palms,
then spilled it free in mirrors,
knitting his secret flowers into song.
This was the only way he knew
to grow into the world, weaving
himself to earth like its shadow,
casting to each object an image
of what it once was, or might be.
He turned blood to rubies, eyes
to planets and moons, and burst
the sun to a psalm of iridescence,
making music visible, and darkness
sing a prophesy of dance.
When his captors tried to follow him,
he led them down a labyrinth
scattered with bluebirds and diamonds.
Then he turned himself so rich and
strange he faded into stars.

All creatures small

What is my boy doing?
He appears to be dancing,
leaping like Pinocchio
from a terrible truth.
Now I see. He is daring
a private quest, not to step
on a single ant
as he makes his way to school.
The ants scatter
like anxious punctuation
as he hops from innocence to
innocence, his heart a clean slate.
Now he is lifting worms with a stick
to place them gently in the grass
where they hide like wide grins.
He wags a finger, chides their careless scrawls.
Birds watch with hungry eyes,
beating their wings at this betrayal.
Scared sacred, the worms cling
to the earth like holy shrines.
Past the school, traffic
vibrates, hums and buzzes
like notorious insects.
His cause is hopeless but undeterred.
He is as sane as sunlight,
pure as the intent of stars.
His war to set this world aright
shames me in my peace.

Bird in the attic

Her wings sweep the pane
as if she knows by instinct
that confinement is a dream
from which she must awaken.
She flutters up and down the pane
searching for answers in the light,
as if a mere entreaty
could shatter an invisible wall.
Now she weaves the huddled space
and slams the pane till her beak turns red.
She cries out in fear against this
encroaching fate, this finite doom.
I tug and pull and yank until
the window opens with an ancient
cry, and she is free, while
my heart flutters madly in its prison.

Call and response

A tree is for thinking
as much as any book is.
When survival is at stake,
roots and branches know.
Trace the top leaves to the stars
until you find the zodiac of fate.
The night sky is skeleton and ghost,
haunted with visions.
Call it a simple attraction
of you and this magnet cosmos,
responsibility of darkness to meteor,
and both to the pull of earth.
Trust your telescope to climb the night.
The stars are sand grain illuminations.
Turn the knob till the past comes clear.
Learn to unfold the light.
Give it time and patience.
Worlds will dream themselves to be.
Stay, stay with the curve of eternity.
Affection is the means, not the end.

Journey with no sound

A hand throws open
a library window
to release the silence.
Freed from words,
it hovers
between drops of rain.
It predicts the dance of leaves,
and it is the patience
the grass keeps.
It comprehends a massacre,
yet the dove, sleeping,
folds it in its cloak.
Between light and darkness
it expands.
It exceeds the hidden wound.
Entering your house,
it inhabits your furniture
and mocks your personal philosophy.
It knows the end
of longing and misery,
and awaits your breath of surrender.

Does the web imagine the spider?

We need not wait for interpretations.
An ant is moving punctuation,
changing the sentence as it goes and goes.
A meaning cannot find itself,
but tree roots spider the earth with clues.
They have learned to clench down deep.
Spider illuminations await the dawn,
as each new web awaits its poem.
Wonder may be a form of patience.
Lucid illusions will find their own fate,
like intricate crickets design the dark.
Watch. Listen.
I follow each longing wind by wind,
the way gaps between stars
whisper the invisible.
It's a matter of precedence.
The wind unwinds the light in things.
There is no leaf that cannot trace the air.
It may be sudden,
this easeful grace,
a silence that surrenders to devotion.

The Madman whirling through the tree

The madman whirling through the tree
scatters the sun's proud abacus
to return the moon to love and madness
and feel psychosis in the stars.
His maddened leaves shimmer the darkness.
His branches weave the havoc in his mind.
The bud within the bloom of fear
irradiates the nerve ends of the stars.
He traces the rain back to angels
until the swirling storm surrenders.
One drop may yet yield a heaven.
He hears the note-less music of the spheres.
Now rains hush fires in his roots
as they probe darkness like moles,
seeking the jewel locked in his heart
that throbs like a gentle star.

The Knitter of Gentle Darkness

A Mexican girl sits knitting
as the night spreads out in dreams,
and old women dream of Autumn winds.
She knits time to space,
warmth to cold, love to
alone, strength to innocence.
She knits moons to their orbits,
needles clicking with the certainty of stars,
webbing the known and unknown.
She knits sweet shadows
that breathe a calm to longing,
and drink the emerald waning of the moon.
Her darkness rounds the world with sleep,
past crouching walls of fearful lands
with the graceful wave of parting lovers.

Agua Nocturna———Octavio Paz

La noche de ojos de cabllo tiemblan en la noche.
La noche de ojos de agua in el campo dormido.
Esta' en tus ojos de caballo que tiembla.
Esta' en tus ojos de agua secreta.
Ojos de agua de sombra,
ojos de agua de pozo,
ojos de agua de sueno.
El silencio y la soledad,
como dos pequenos animals a quienes guis la luna,
beben en esos ojos,
beben en esas aguas.
Si abres los ojos,
si abre la nohe de puertas de musgo,
se abre el reino secreto del agua
que mana del centro de la noche.
Y si los cierras,
un rio, una corriente dulce y silenciosa,
te inunda por dentro, avanza, te hace obscura,
la noche moja reberas en tu alma.

Nocturnal water — — —By Octavio Paz

The night with the eyes of the horse trembling in the night
The night with eyes of water in the sleeping field.
It is in your eyes of a trembling horse.
It is in your eyes of secret water.
Eyes of the shadow's water,
eyes of the well's water,
eyes of the water of dreams.
Silence and solitude,
like two small animals guided by the moon,
drink from those eyes,
drink from those waters.
If you open your eyes,
The night opens its doors of moss,
opens the secret kingdom of water
that flows from the center of night.
If you close them,
a river, a sweet and silent current,
floods over you from within, moves over your shadow.
Night soaks the riverbanks in your soul.

My father's cat

My father kept
an abandoned cat
inside him,
both fatherless
in this land of disconnections.
I watched it glide into his heart
each night,
clawing every silence till it bled.
I watched him swallow his own shadow
to feed it. It purred like a spun revolver.
A walking shadow,
it hunted through his veins
in search of madness to stroke and nurture,
haunted his nights with proper rage,
chilled his insomnia bones to zero.
Its claws clenched tight round all his nightmares
as it howled in loneliness and despair.
I hid on those nights. I feared that thing
inside him, that knew no end to hunger.
When he died it finally left him
as he left it, empty of reasons.
And now at night it cries for me,
and I follow it down endless alleys,
searching for the father they never found.

The wolf as original dreamer

The earth would burst incandescent,
they said, but I was prepared
with an army of dreams and magic,
and each night a thousand stars
descended from the ceiling like cobalt spiders
to weave my bed of innocence.
The fall came when my father placed a book
of Peter and the Wolf before the mirror.
I could not stop watching the wolf,
its lava eyes spilling rage and violation,
its teeth swirling in a snarl of white death,
its feet clawing for the earth to return.
Above, Peter clung to the tree branch
faceless, like all sadists,
tightening the noose over its tail
to suspend it through eternity,
and to make the torture exquisite,
he made music from its misery.
Tonight, alone in bed,
my wife dying, son grown and gone,
the wolf leaps from a shadow in my dream,
folds itself around me, shredded tail bleeding.
I sing gently to it,
sharing the hunger still hovering in the air.

Nominated for the Pushcart Prize for Poetry, 2006

Other mysterious worlds

Other mysterious worlds redeem our own,
when we dream we are alone.
When the touch of a loving hand
shatters the mind's glass,
and renders us as breathless as a star.
Then we see the planets are mere seeds
strung from an endless longing.
We learn the language of loneliness,
love's strange and fateful equations,
and surrender's sweet song beneath the covers.
Only mysterious worlds will do,
when oblivion's eye is too all-knowing,
the light years a cry of pain can weave,
or the beauty of a withered hand
no more reconciled to alone.

Shadow heart

I need to return
to my first shadow,
which embraced me,
and taught me the sweetness of night.
We come, stunned by the invisible
into life. Turn back, heart,
be true to the lost perfection
of a mosquito drinking dew.
What are these hands but shattered flames,
meant to caress the stars? Open, my heart,
to the suffering of stones, the swan questioning
silence, the Word dreaming of the rose.

Part Two: The Other as Salvation

"Hell is other people"

—Jean Paul Sartre, *No Exit*

"What is hell? Hell is oneself.
Hell is alone, the other figures in it
merely projections."

—T.S. Eliot, *The Cocktail Party*

Random photograph

It's the two in the background
who interest me.
A young woman, brunette, pretty,
in plain cloth coat. Holding
her hand, a girl, say—eight?
a violin case clutched in her free hand.
They might be sisters.
They are not the focus of the shot.
Imagine: She takes lessons
from a superb concert violinist
currently in need of work.
Imagine: The older one is well-
educated, was once in love,
yet something is gone in her eyes.
Perhaps a childhood dream
of studying art in Vienna.
Perhaps a loss within a loss?
It's hard to tell in the world of the gone.
The man is the camera's intention.
Tall, blonde. Eyes like a ferret.
Say he's wealthy. Look at those
perfect, half-moon fingernails!
Double-breasted suit of charcoal flannel,
ring on his pinky, must by crystal blue.
So he's wealthy then. He's speaking
silence. His mouth forever open.
Imagine: He's a businessman. All business.
Money in furs. But mostly synthetic rubber
these days. Started with ashtrays,

then expanded into affluence.
His name? Gunther sounds good.
But it's the others who draw me in—
nameless, barely in view.
headed somewhere perhaps un-nameable.
I found the photograph in a rummage sale,
lining the bottom of a box.
Owner: Unknown No names.
On back: "Leipzig, 1937."

The daguerreotype's unanswered questions

I found my high school yearbook.
I'm the only one not smiling.
Even the chess club and audio-visual crew
are smiling. And I know that's not true.
These smiles seem forgeries, clenched in fear or aggression,
seeking something to bluff or grind,
snails and sharks in turtlenecks and tiaras.
Was the photo portrait always this way?
Here's a photograph of Anna Dostoevsky,
1863. She is not smiling.
She looks back through the lens to me,
as if demanding a response.
And here is Emily Dickinson,
her eyes like glittering blades,
her fingers worrying a flower to a rage.
You see what she thinks of this smiling business.
And now a family daguerreotype
my father found in an abandoned farmhouse.
Not one smile, not even the baby.
Were they heartless, soulless, these chiaroscuro ghosts?
Were their lives as hard as their stares?
Or was life serious enough to them to be lived?
Soulful, patient, like a soaked image coming clear,
or a prayer that penetrates the stars.
I long to hear this other world of shades,
to pour my blood and draw them into speech.
But the chasm is great. The dark brings no relief.
The answers fall and break like Winter leaves.

Diamond of Silence

Mr. Winegarden fought in two wars,
one West, one East,
and when he returned home,
he never said one word.
Our baseball diamond had no home,
a brick for first base, a shed for second,
and a clothesline pole for third,
mumbling with bitter bumblebees.
It was Mr. Winegarden's yard.
He watched us play but never said one word,
cocked back on a wooden poker chair,
whiskey bottle at his feet.
One day he broke that old shed down
with a sledgehammer, yanked out the
pole, bashed it to bits and burned it.
The bees whirled off like discarded planets.
He painted lines in smooth and straight,
placed three bases, soft and safe as pillows,
then home, molded and packed a pitcher's mound,
then returned to his chair and whiskey.
On that silent diamond we played baseball
the only way to play baseball—for eternity,
for golden summers and the blue within
the blue, no need to even keep score.
Nights he stretched out on the mound,
watching the moon displace the darkness.
Still he said nothing. Perhaps the silence
had forgotten what it once longed to say.

Inheritance

In the back of my grandmother's antique store
I overhear my grandfather chanting:
"I don't want to die. I'm afraid to die,"
and my grandmother soothes him, "I know, I know."
And she opens, opens doors, drapes, blinds and windows,
old glass lights in carillon colors,
and still he cries his fear of dying.
But I am five and the watches are asleep.
Clocks line the walls, each hushed at a separate hour.
This store is a theater of light,
crystal air, tobacco scents, and hard-bound
books, clasping secret knowledge.
And now her hands guide me to the garden,
and I am all lit crystal and sun,
as the world rehearses another day.
The light stings like shattered glass,
and broken strings are blowing in the trees.

Double shift

Even when he worked a double shift
at the plant, my father gave me night rides,
his shoulders strong, weighted with time.
He carried me up to another world
of breezes and branches. Weightless,
I became all reaching hand and air.
The sky crayoned purple, the moon
a pleasant zero, content and
whole in silver.
A space between the trees opened
with a gentle stirring, revealing
stars and planets, patient, waiting.
So briefly, the interlocking gears
of the sky—paused—their labors,
time's punch clock frozen for now.
My legs clenched round his neck,
leaves lowering like medals
I would pin on him if I could.

The watcher in the window

Each night my father took a factory home
under his fingernails, in his clothes and hair…
Westinghouse Electric,
always the great bruised clouds
that came like immense wings
over blue, forgotten hills,
over the cowering town,
their shadows dropping into streets
like umbrellas with broken spines.
I waited each night at the upstairs window,
watching the pulsating sky. The distant
factory leered at the night with slouched
hat and loveless cigarette. I watched the
Standard Oil fireball, blood sun of night,
watched for my father's headlights
probing the last turn,
bringing certainty home.
I watched the moonbeams
spill from branch to branch.
Did his bones ache like the depths of oceans?
Did his ghosted breath release his wounds?
Did he feel under his cracked boot soles
the worm's breath whispering constellations?
I never knew. But I knew the stars
conspired the silence
for this watcher in the window

Capturing the light

You need to capture the light,
my father tells me, and he knows,
for he has captured it many times,
to let it go.
I see and learn. The light
is a cabbage moth, here, there,
forever uncertain and vulnerable,
alighting from image to image.
His goal is the wild canary,
and suddenly I see
it is the only bird to him,
its mustard wings the only yellow.
She rests cupped within the wheat,
swaying with the autumn wind.
She sees only gold, and sun and
happiness, and not him at all.
My father moves with the grace of a breeze
that barely disturbs the wheat.
His feet leave no track in the grass.
Breathless, he bends light like a prism.
He has become
a stencil, a parenthesis,
a turning lens that turns
the world round with it.
And now they are one,
bird and image of bird,
light and the wheat that spins it gold,
everything bright with eternity.

My father's light

Hands carry them up from the basement
of the art studio, for the showing.
My father's photographs,
each one glowing with captured light,
a moment held above the flow.
"The picture is not in you," he told me,
"nor in the camera. It's within the object seen."
I remember his light meter clicking
like a radioactive cricket.
I can feel his hands
on my shoulders, his breath on my head.
"Capture the light. All of it."
And the camera lens widening,
feeding on light and color.
And now his images rise,
more and more alighting,
a shifting prism of possible worlds,
the luminous air knowing itself
at last. His visions
crowd sofas, occupy desks
and chairs, fill all the walls,
until the whole room is a sun
of incandescent time.

Kite-flying at night

My hand in yours, cupped in,
feels like another's, yours like mine,
as we let the string race out
like hourglass sand in reverse.
Holding on, letting go, joy
ripples through our fingers,
then takes our breath skywards
to climb the vibrant stars.
The kite quivers at first
a no, then turns, shy, half-
yielding, a yes, begins the dance,
touching a graceful wind
that whispers through the trees.
It peers at islands we can only dream
below, our backs cool and slippery.
We trust love inch by inch until
with a last sliver of surrender,
the moon,
remembering who we are,
gently lifts us home.

Oh willow, willow

It was raining keys,
but someone had stolen the doors.
Then you came again,
eyes that knew right through me,
hands like moons caressing shores,
thirsting sand, piano surf,
bell sky, snail clouds,
floating spiders webbing desire,
sun-drenched hair of the willow,
and my outcast breaths craving grace.
And you, acrobat of touch,
like a perdu gull, far, far,
whispered light to life, all night now
sewn deep beneath the stars,
and broken castles rooted in the sand,
throbbing veins, spent skin,
and hearts, hearts, no more within.
Fold me love, into your hands.
Teach me the persistence of imagined wings.

I love the whole world, which includes your left shoulder

I only ask
our every breath
spend itself to ecstasy
and that all
my echoes
lose themselves in your hair.
And so
I love the whole world,
which includes your left shoulder
and whatever else
within or without
you care to reveal or share.
We are both
the ones within
each other.
The only ghosts for me
drink the longing of icicles
melting in the sun.
Let's dance our skeletons free
and then, naked at last,
shed the nakedness too.
Let us sink down and down,
depth through the earth
to the good human bone of love.
Your left shoulder
knows what I mean
more than all the libraries.

Her nightgowns

Her gold reveals the mind's impoverishment
next to the body's guiding contours,
her slink and lace more delicate, more sure
than any man's naked computations.
Her black gown shimmers with possibility,
for what covers, reveals, the way darkness
shivers the stars awake, and mystery
depends on the clues that hide and seek.
Her white is not what you're thinking,
no virgin snows or angels wings for her.
White helps her dream of waterspouts
that guide the wave to summer rain.
Purple is the color of her breakdown
from mourning,
when retreating night and silk of love
proved the holiness of tears.
When she whirls in her green,
she comes, she comes imagining
old dead Winter back to Spring,
and still she keeps a secret of her name.
In blue she triumphs all the male,
for blue subdues him, tames his wars,
turns his baboon soul to evolution,
and haunts his heart with moons that dream of dawn.

The obscenity of angels

Copley Health Care Center.
My wife, thirty-seven, waits
while her Multiple Sclerosis
patiently possesses her brain
like an old cat circling a dying fire.

"I can't remember my name."
"Sue. It's Sue.
"Where was I born?"
I write her name and age
inside a copy of *Moby Dick*.
"I could never finish that book."
"It's all right. The whale wins."
I have to breathe,
if only for a moment.
I excuse myself, seek
the sunlit labyrinth of the halls,
that are bathed in antiseptics.
I see old men with feet big as lobsters,
question marks in wheelchairs,
and women with hands that quiver
like brutalized birds.
I return, and she says:
"I don't remember…"
"Don't worry."
"I don't understand things anymore."
"Shhhhh…"
I press the book into her hand and smile.
I want to annihilate all the books,

offer their creators
hypodermic crucifixions.
I want no more words to hurt her.

Her breaths come softly now,
like leaves tumbling to confusion,
and an old cat,
fully-fed,
curls gently in a sunlit chair
and goes to sleep.

Awakening the abyss

The first moment of awakening,
seagull balanced on a wave,
ecstasy and nightmare,
asleep in the belly of a dove.
And memory—
the clutch of raspberry branches
whose leaves folded like prayer.
Those tiny bruises she pressed into my mouth,
blood of life
once, so long ago,
joy found me without searching.
When her hands, clenched in mine,
dubbed me skeptic of stones,
and clothed my bones in grassy flesh.
Our breaths carved the sky with moons,
and love, breathlessly past persuasion,
needed no more words.
Lost between night and morning,
I had forgotten her grave nearby,
and with a terrified cry of the sun,
heaven and hell embraced
and became the sobbing earth.
Deep beneath these covers,
her fading still clings like a desperate birth.

'To despair

Deprive my lavender ghosts of darkness,
and they will learn to dance the dawn.
or touch the soothing rhythm of the stars.
Scatter my leaves to merely guessing,
and I will guide their winds to meaning.
A single leaf can autograph the air.
Stranger my soul to cliff side,
and I will cast the darkest thoughts away.
I'm no stranger to what death may dream.
No ill wind can end my longing
for nights when shadows learn their names,
as earth longs for heaven's reign,
the sea longs free from moon's tyranny,
or rivers seek deep through inner earth,
chanting its heart to prayer.

Part Three: From Walt Whitman's America to Donald Trump's America

"For starting westward from Hindustan,

From the vales of Kashmere,

From Asia, from the north, from the god, the sage, the hero…

Now I face home again, very pleas'd and joyous.

But where is what I started for so long ago?

And why is it yet unfound?

—Walt Whitman, "Facing West from California's Shores"

Walt Whitman at the game

Walt Whitman,
containing multitudes,
spreads his plump rump on the bleachers,
his blooming beard caressed by diamond breezes.
The umpire raises one hand in benediction.
The batter swings and swings at nothing,
then cocks a grin as wide as a blind assumption.
The ball soars, high, higher,
seeking the looming towers of Manhattan,
angels or demons,
catchers and pitchers of the winds.
In Walt's eye, the ball, a polished moon,
folds into a dove recalling home.
Cheers wound the sky in its envy.
The grass burns the blades of its desire.
Walt Whitman absorbs it all
in the visionary marrow of his bones,
scents the fisted rosin, the silky dust,
touches the joy of the pulsing sun,
weaves the crowd with his eyes
into a pattern of his own design.
Later, he dances home, arm in-
arm with two drunken firemen,
following a trail of apples
that have abandoned their fall.
Above, a thousand windows embrace the sun,
and in wonder's perfect silence, Walt Whitman drinks
and drinks the city night, sprinkled with blood and wine
immaculate, breathless in the ministry of stars.

The Eyes of Leo Frank

Witness complicity, prisoned in eyes.
Look for yourself, and see yourself seeing.
Accuse "truth," wrung from a thousand lies.
How redeem the time without redreaming?
The crime they screamed was never mine.
On her body they found a note:
"My name is Mary Phagan. I live
at 146 Lindsey Street." A whole life
held in one short page.
Twelve cents an hour, thirteen years old,
money for school,
her people forgotten, work to afford hope.
The tragedy was her death, not my trial.
Tragedy is time. I was dead
before the first gavel banged.
The Temperance ladies cast their bones,
and sat down to evening tea,
then rocked to sleep in gentle homes,
an old nightmare, dreaming me.
I saw my accuser, Jim Conley.
I died for him, his eyes died for me,
knowing what I knew,
innocence and guilt wedded in a glance.
I saw their eyes, all, all their eyes,
magic eyes, conjuring monsters from clouds,
eyes pooled with hate to drown the mind.
I heard their voices,
their words of hate glinting
in the night's cloak. The strongest

voices cried for sacrifice.
I knew you all,
I knew the hate pulsing your hearts
was purer than all love,
and far more deadly than truth.

The sheriff who tied my hands
dubbed me "Nigger Jew."
The judge who drove the wagon
was a Little League umpire.
The minister who draped the noose
blessed me in Jesus's name,
and the man who tied the blindfold,
so gently, I had known for years.
In a blind world, hearts in tombs,
death alone brings awe,
and when the night dropped down to doom,
I saw, and saw, and saw…

Makley

Charles Makley, orphan,
adopted by aunt and uncle,
farmers, their hands were hard,
their lives were hard,
the bank had half their land.
For two days the boy said nothing,
staring at hard things—
their floor, their shoes, their land.
The aunt said: "Watch our hogs for us."
So he watched the hogs.
He was the hog watcher.
He watched their snouts, big as fists,
their hard, certain hooves,
their round, shameless shanks,
their eyes like hard peas,
and ears like pink paper hats.
He stroked their sandpaper backs
and spoke softly to them
as they nudged their heads into the craven earth.
One day, his uncle took a huge shovel
and slammed it between a hog's eyes.
Its head caved in like a mound of earth,
then it sank to its knees as if in prayer,
and kicked itself loose from its life.
The boy's eyes darkened and turned inward.
He had not known what a hog farmer is.
Now he knew.
He ran, and when they found him

caught in the barb wire, they carried him home
and bathed him in Jesus and Datalatum.

Years later, he rode with Dillinger,
bashing banks and sheriffs,
winking at the snout-nosed bankers,
making them all pay.
His hands were murders,
his eyes violations.
9-22-34:
Scheduled for execution,
at the Ohio State Pen,
he made a break for it,
but he had grown too fat,
and could not make the gate.
When they shot him in the barb wire,
he dangled for a moment,
one hand stroking the back of the wind.

Robert Lowell shops at Sears

Fans with streamers tranquilize the air.
Toasters whisper to washing machines
and ovens open wide, longing to devour
Robert Lowell as he ventures into Sears,
glasses blooming with florescent angels.
The store hums with a vast production,
a hydrogen Levittown, like weapons on display.
He pays, lifts his future over his head.
Longing for a stopwatch for his fear,
Robert Lowell goes wading into time.
Tate wrote: 'My house is full of profs and poets.
You'd have to pitch a tent." He was kidding.
Lowell is not kidding. He has come to pitch
a Sears Roebuck Nashville Special on Tate's lawn,
so he may be somewhere anywhere home.
He memorizes the directions, then
improvises, and only with the last
driven stake do his fingers stop shaking.
Here he will act his pen and penance
for a past that haunts him like a hungry grave.
He will make a sound space here, no heir
or ancestor to thunder No. The stars
will bless him, the apples feed him, and
Sears Roebuck keep a craft within him,
even when madness creeps through the grass.

Grandfather Story

Here's a photograph—
My mother, six, her father,
sitting in a horse-drawn cart,
Greeley Chapel Road
outside his general store,
1922.
Summer Fridays they'd arrive home late
from the county market,
pass the fairgrounds.
My mother would ask:
"Who are those people there, celebrating?"
And he would reply: "Oh, that. That's
The Idiot's Convention."
And my mother would always wonder
why all the idiots would meet
at the Fair at the same time,
light crosses, chant songs,
alighting on the Ferris wheel
like departing spirits rising,
only to be returned.
Helpless to break the wall
of love my Grandfather
wove from lie and truth.

Charlie Parker Negative

No trickster god,
demon, savior, saint or
train wreck, but human, very.
Not irrational, primal,
primitive, dark unconscious,
exile or martyr.
No more priapic
than your Sunday morning
erection. Not lost or "liminal."
There are no "Negro Streets,"
no heroin angels or
lavender moons of despair.
No lilac evenings, no metaphors.
They all went bust, and all
is not well, not well at all.
No "pure instinct." But
fifteen hours practice a day,
and love might begin again.

The Blue Note Diner, 1965

"I don't serve niggers,"
the waitress said calmly,
and left, taking my last words
with her on her note pad.
I was twelve, white, speechless
as empty paper. That word
could not touch me, though.
Only one word.
But that word had entered my friend, Nathan,
and taken a world with it.
It had entered his very center, done dire work.
His black fingers shivered in the frozen air.
He covered his face and cried.
Why was I still whole?
Anger flowed through my blood and fists,
but a wounded bird fluttered in his heart.
How did he see this petty woman?
Was she ten feet tall to him?
A world without, a world within,
need not be the same.
Now I knew, now I knew,
as I tried in vain to console him—
the power and emptiness of words,
the terrible solitude of a soul.

Night fishing in Hog River

Awaken, Lima, Ohio,
and wait for the sun
to carve with its bloody wand
this winding, mysterious wound
through the forsaken heart of your city.
Once it held bold herons
that perched like sentinels
to guard the innocence of wonder.
Now it bends uncertainly
past the banks of its lost imaginings.
It flows tonight, barely,
past steel and iron factories
lined like abandoned battleships,
curls past Meat City, its broken banks
littered with torn lottery tickets.
Watch as it becomes a snake of mirrors
that shivers the knives of stars
past your houses blinded with despair,
evicted furniture piled high
as if lives were merely some excretion.
Far down a lonely bend,
a Black boy is fishing for visions
under a stuck tambourine moon,
but all he pulls from the depths of dreams
is the silence of unraveled stars.
He searches, keyless, for a door in the night,
and now he's knocking everywhere,
on visions old, and the countless air,

through solstices of solitude,
and on his heart, to prove it's there.

Ohio angel with rusted wings,
look down to your child.
Teach him, guide him, show him
his hands were not made for hunger,
but to find a sustenance within.
If not, he'll have nothing but this lost river,
and the wind's empty hand
will keep him always
a Black boy outside a locked door,
counting his lures down to despair.

The Racist's Credo

I hate people like that.
I hate people like.
I hate people.
I hate.
I.

End Men Blues

Moon and Stars,
Tambo and Bones,
ritual darkness,
degradation in alone
like moonlit knives in a lynching.
The wind has learned
to disguise its voice,
and the bloody eye of Mars
pretends it cannot see.
The Blues are pure Black,
not white.
There is no coward
like a shotgun,
no question
stranger than a noose.
No ignorance
that cannot learn to hate.
To be a man,
yet feel yourself hunted,
or whispered to oblivion,
to hear footsteps
that track you through the night
like radioactive panthers.
Emmet Till
to Ahmaud Arbery, George Floyd,
watch the darkness mirror you,
and every day
is Golgotha
rightly seen.

Greyhound Iowa Refugee

In this bus station,
white as phosphorus,
a black saxman
floats through the air with apocalypse Blues.
Outside, catatonic stoplights,
wires strung from some
central black widow spider,
seem to watch only me.
The bus arrives, silver and sulphur,
exhausted, steams and sighs.
I am now a suspicious character,
with a fake i.d. and Aztec eyes.
I don't want to murder you,
or the world. I only want
to eat, to breathe free,
to follow an old dream.
I've made it North, far North,
hoping the fear might freeze.
But high in the blue, vigilant jets
crucify the sky.
Why do they hate eternity?
Hate it, the closer it comes?
Why do I fear these eyes
pressed round me in the dark?

And when Buddy Holly dreamed
the corn, was this the dream
he died to awaken, on that blind night
when the stars tumbled down?

Orphan Day at the Science Marina

No Rachel calls their names
as they stare in wonder at the trapped fish,
the fish that hover in their home of eternal rain,
float like magical plums and pears
of heaven, in their prison,
unfurl their cavalry plumes
or descend in silken surrender,
swell to the size of medallions
or melt into ripples of light and melody,
fins silently whirring.
The children's voices treble the glass
as they watch these radiant coins
tossed here from another dimension,
trembling in phosphorescent recognition
of the lost, trapped in the alcoholic stare
of the aquariums, the mystery of loss,
sunk beneath the bones of the city.
The children crave the way the fish swim
in their wealth, the way their gold
and silver darts carve the light,
their obsidian eyes keeping some secret
even from themselves.
And now, through the ultramarine shimmer,
other creatures appear. These are human.
Silk suits and lavender gloves,
dutiful ties and smiles, careless, flowing
dresses—the Benefactors, "wise guardians
of the poor," fresh from the honeyed trees
of Lake Forest. Their eyes watch the

same old shark, same old shark, in his
buried sea involved with revolving eyes.

Only the children and their lonely fish
know the deep throbbing vacancy of hunger,
hunger for space, for light, for stars that remember,
for anything real that can smash this kingdom
of glass and despair, so that the children,
freed from pity, might seek their lost
mothers' cries, and the fish, freed from science,
float to the seas of the feathered skies.

Midwest photographs

Railroads collapsed
arteries, factories
abandoned beehives.
Broken bridges, ghost hotels,
a man who sells balloons
in all the colors of memory.
A sign: Gas,
cigs, lottery,
beer.
A drunk outside
The Utopia Bar
sings of lost kingdoms.
Beneath Yankee skies,
Confederate flags
for sale.
An old Black man
bends to retrieve
a lucky penny.
Schools named Liberty,
Freedom and Hope.
Children enslaved to despair.
Morning dew,
blood and rust,
tighten your belt another notch.
Disease in the air.
And masks. You can't tell
the robbers from the robbed.
Now our people
peer through windows

and steal moments from each other's lives.
Life goes on
in another town,
another room, always.

Charlottesville

Fever hangs in the willows.
The man with the cocksure eye
awaits you down this road.
Trees spell their leaves in syllables of fear.
A black ghost and a white ghost
dance a mystery through your past.
Read these August birds, crossed in winds.
A death may carve you mystic,
or leave you chanting in the dust.
The kid with an engine for a heart
has one dream alone,
to give misery its own last name.
The man with the cocksure eye
was General Someone once,
but something's buried beneath his marble.
Beware his phantom statue,
as it cries for the corpse of Honor,
and sinks into the silence of the swamp.
And beware this grieving yesteryear.
Its land lies purge-less in its blood.
And its dead walk torch-lit in the night.

Make America Great Again

The house is a shrug with cataract windows.
A wall surrounds it, broken with fears.
Out back there's someone in a cage.
There's an attic where a scream abides,
a grandfather clock chock full of secrets.
A mob is coming up the road.
Father Shotgun's in his rocker.
Aunt Shivers glares her hypodermic eyes
at the mourners she sees hiding in the mirror.
Rusted through, the stoveheart of this house.
The television glows in cancer blue,
the floorboards spreading red a stain.
The mother, pock-marked in hate,
sings Amazing Grace so she won't faint.
Outside, torches chant the night.
The Deputy descends to the cellar,
his flashlight a halo in Hell.
The time has come, there's no escape…
There's someone in the doorway taking notes.

Pulling out the corpse

It's coming now, coming out in screams.
Keep pulling on your heart, it is there,
somewhere deep inside the poison.
Now here's the mouth, working blindly
like a gasping fish. Words ring free of it,
spilling like stolen gold to the floor.
Pull harder, deeper, unroll the shadows,
reels and reels of radioactive night
that explode in black and blue flies.
It resists your every effort,
clinging to memories in your blood,
sucking the marrow from your bones.
It wants your every breath for dying,
its eyes as empty as a mannequin's,
as cold as the silence between a child's cries.
Here it is at last!—that gelid, soul-less
mold of you, that sees nothing, feels nothing.
It slides to the floor like an afterbirth.
Stare directly at its wretched face
until it no more claims complicity.
See beneath it to the king of lies.
The burial comes later.
A yew tree longs to plug its filthy mouth.

Coda

"Thou art That."

—-Chandogya Upanishad

Placing a stone

I am here in the Jewish graveyard
on the cheap land
next to the Catholic graveyard,
both near a junkyard,
the wealthy Protestants high and far away.
Home towns are stable, but they never learn.
Here where the lost cry silence to the rain,
I come to place a stone.
Here where headstones whisper their names,
I kneel to time and mystery.
Does the world feel its own embrace?
The trees cast their leaves to wound the Fall.
Somehow the wind knows the way home.
My friend lies here where nothing hurts again.

The Dead Know No Circumference

Butterfly shadows are souls of the dead,
tracing their flight with darkness.
Butterfly patterns unravel the wind,
and the dead know no circumference.
What is buried will always rise again,
like red sums in your hidden accounts.
Our sins whisper the accusing air,
and the dead know no circumference.
Auschwitz children dream painted butterflies
that inscribe the air with love.
Their souls are ashes that rise to the sun,
and the dead know no circumference.

Commission

I have a commission from eternity
to capture all syllables that bleed,
and march them in a wounded line
till darkness learns to see.
I have a commission from eternity
to put my mind in peril,
and find the lie wound round each truth,
the pain round every pearl.
I have a commission from eternity
to speak Sybil to the Earl,
to warn him of his numbered days,
and her leaves spelled round the world.
I have a commission from eternity
to learn secrets from the wind,
and cast them round in words so sound,
no alone may find again.